"I cannot think of anything more important for a child to know than the fact that God delights to hear their prayers — especially when those prayers are grounded in Scripture. This resource is going to help families and children learn that God loves it when we pray the truths in his word back to him."

J.T. English, Lead Pastor, Storyline Church, Arvada, Colorado; Author of *Deep Discipleship* and *You Are a Theologian*

"Vibrant prayers are informed by God's word and fueled by his promises. Using *God's Big Promises Bible Story Prayers* with your children can help them get into the rhythm of responding to God's word through prayer even before they can read. It's never too early for children to learn to respond to God's great and precious promises through prayer!"

Betsy Childs Howard, Editor, The Gospel Coalition; Author of *Arlo and the Great Big Cover-Up*

"Here is a great and faithful way to engage precious little minds and hearts that every parent, grandparent, relative and friend can use. This wonderful resource will help children share in prayers of praise, thanksgiving, confession and petition, using words and ideas that are just right for them (and — say it quietly — just right for grown-ups too!)."

Adrian Reynolds, Head of National Ministries, FIEC, UK

"Learning to pray the Bible changed the way I talk to God. I'm thankful for a resource that will help my kids learn to pray Scripture much sooner than I did!"

Hunter Beless, Founder of Journeywomen Ministries; Author of *Read It, See It, Say It, Sing It!* and *Amy Carmichael: The Brown-Eyed Girl Who Learned to Pray*

"Prayer is a privilege... and it can be hard. That's why written prayers are a gift to the whole church, and I love how this resource offers this gift to our kids. Each prayer is simple enough that a child can understand it yet rich enough to stir their hearts (and ours) with God's amazing truth. My kids will love this!"

Kristen Wetherell, Author of the For the Bible Tells Me So board book series and *Hope When It Hurts*

God's Big Promises Bible Story Prayers I © The Good Book Company 2024

thegoodbook.com I thegoodbook.co.uk I thegoodbook.com.au I thegoodbook.co.nz I thegoodbook.co.in

Unless otherwise indicated, Scripture references are quoted from the International Children's Bible®, copyright ©1986, 1988, 1999, 2015 by Tommy Nelson. Used by permission.

Where indicated (NIV), Scripture references are taken from the Holy Bible, New International Version. Copyright © 2011 Biblica, Inc.TM. Used by permission.

Illustrations by Jennifer Davison I Design and Art Direction by André Parker

ISBN: 9781802541045 I JOB-007616 I Printed in India

GOD'S **BIG** PROMISES
Bible Story
Prayers

Written by
Carl Laferton

Illustrated by
Jennifer Davison

CONTENTS

WELCOME

HOW TO USE THIS BOOK

God made every star in the sky. God gives every beat to our hearts. And this God hears us as we talk to him.

That's *amazing!*

When we pray, God promises to listen to us.
When we pray, God promises to give us what we need.
And the Bible shows us that God always keeps his promises.

When you have a conversation with someone, you listen to them and you speak to them. It's just the same with God. Prayer is us speaking to God, and the Bible is God speaking to us. So it's great to pray in response to what we hear in the Bible.

In this book, you'll find 92 prayers that are each linked to a summary of and a verse from a Bible story. These prayers will take you all the way from beginning to end of the true story of the Bible – from Genesis to Revelation. And at the end of this book, you'll find nine prayers that are perfect for praying at bedtime.

Right at the back is an index, helping you quickly turn to prayers that are particularly helpful in moments or feelings that most of us — children and grown-ups — experience as we go through life.

Each prayer links with a Bible story in the God's Big Promises Bible Storybook. So you can use these prayers after you've read the story from the Bible Storybook, or you can use them at a different time of the day. Or you can use this book on its own.

One more thing: every prayer in this book contains one or more of these types of prayers:

- **Praise** prayers, where we praise God for how great he is. We can call these 'Wow!' prayers.

- **Thank you** prayers, where we thank God for what he's done or will do for us.

- **Sorry** prayers, where we say sorry to God for the things we've done that are wrong.

- **Please** prayers, where we ask God for his help.

Each of these types of prayers – Wow, Thank you, Sorry, and Please – are marked in a **different type of writing**. And each comes with its own action to do with your body, if you'd like to:

Wow

Thank you

Sorry

Please

That will help everyone join in with the prayer as it's read aloud.

Being able to pray to God really is amazing. God promises that if we are followers of Jesus, he'll listen to us in the same way that a great dad listens to his children. And, as the Bible story tells us over and over again, God always keeps all of his promises!

GOD'S **BIG** PROMISES

Prayers
based on
The Old Testament

In the Beginning

In the beginning, God made everything. The best thing God made was a man and a woman to be friends with him and take care of the world. It was all very good.

The Bible says, "God created human beings in his image … He created them male and female. God blessed them."

(Genesis chapter 1 verses 27-28)

Dear God,
You made the stars and the mountains, the seas and the rivers. **Wow!**
You made all the fish and birds and every plant and every animal, including the ones I love the most! **Wow!**
You made everything from nothing.
I praise you for your power and imagination.
Thank you, God, most of all, for making me. Amen.

In the Garden

God gave the first people a wonderful garden to live in. They could enjoy life with God forever. There was just one tree that God told them not to eat from – the tree that showed who was in charge.

"The Lord God commanded [the man], 'You may eat the fruit from any tree in the garden. But you must not eat the fruit from the tree which gives the knowledge of good and evil.'" (Genesis 2:16-17)

Dear God,
We know that you are in charge of this world.
You always know what is best for us, because you made us.
Thank you that you put so many good things in this world for us to enjoy. **Thank you** that you give us good rules that help us enjoy everything.
Please keep reminding us that your ways are always best. Amen.

The Snake and the Tree

Adam and Eve listened to the snake instead of to God. They decided to disobey God, and ate from the tree God had told them not to eat from. But they did not feel as happy as they had before.

"The woman ... took some of its fruit and ate it. She also gave some of the fruit to her husband who was with her, and he ate it."

(Genesis 3:6)

Dear God,
It is sad that the first people chose to disobey you instead of loving and obeying you.
Sometimes we are tempted to do the same thing.
Sometimes we think that disobeying you will be good. But it never is.
So, we are **sorry** for the times when we don't obey you.
Thank you that you always love us, even when we disobey you. Amen.

Out of the Garden

Because Adam and Eve had sinned by not loving and obeying God, they could not enjoy life with God forever. But God promised that one day someone would put everything right again.

"The payment for sin is death. But God gives us the free gift of life forever in Christ Jesus our Lord."

(Romans 6:23)

Dear God,
The world has gone wrong because people sin.
I am **sorry** for the ways that I sin by not loving and obeying you.
Thank you that you can forgive me and help me do the right thing next time.
Thank you for promising us that one day Jesus will put everything right again!
Thank you that you always keep your promises.
Amen.

Noah Builds an Ark

God told Noah to build a huge boat so that he would be safe when God sent a flood. Noah believed God's promise, so he did as God said. When the flood came, God kept Noah's family safe in the ark.

"Noah did everything that God commanded him." (Genesis 6:22)

Dear God,
Thank you that you warned Noah about the flood.
Thank you that you told him to build a boat.
Thank you that you speak to me in the Bible to help me know what to do, too. Your commands are always good and right. **Thank you** that I can trust you when you tell me what to do.
Please help me to listen to you and obey you, just like Noah did.
Amen.

The First Rainbow

God rescued Noah and his family from the flood. He promised never to flood the world again, and put a rainbow in the sky as a reminder of his promise.

"God said to Noah, 'That rainbow is a sign. It is the sign of the agreement that I made with all living things on earth.'"

(Genesis 9:17)

Dear God,
Thank you that you rescued Noah and his family from the flood, just as you had promised.
Thank you that you have made promises to me.
You have promised to love me and look after me.
You have promised to forgive me if I ask you to.
You always keep your promises. **Wow!**
Please remind me of that whenever I see a rainbow in the sky.
Amen.

The Tall Tower

People worked together to disobey God. They built a tower to show how great they were. God stopped them building, so that they would spread out and fill the world, just as he had planned.

"The Lord scattered them from there over all the earth. And they stopped building the city. That is where the Lord confused the language of the whole world."

(Genesis 11:8-9)

Dear God,
You have a good plan to make sure that there are people all over the world who love and obey you.
Thank you that your good plans always happen and that no one can stop them.
Thank you for people who have gone to live in other countries so that they can spread the news about you there. **Please** give them bravery and energy.
Today, right now, **please** cause more people in more countries to become your friends. Amen.

God's Promises to Abram

God promised Abram a huge family and a good land to live in. They would live under God's rule and be happy. God promised to use Abram's family to bring that happiness to people all over the world. Abram believed God.

"Then the Lord said to Abram, 'Leave your country, your relatives and your father's family. Go to the land I will show you.
I will make you a great nation, and I will bless you …
And all the people on earth will be blessed through you.'"

(Genesis 12:1-3)

Dear God,
You make big promises, and you keep your big promises.
Thank you that you have promised us that you will always love us, that you are with us, and that all your people will enjoy life with you forever.
Please help us believe your promises, just as Abram believed the promises you gave him.
Please help us to obey you, just like Abram obeyed you.
Please help us to show people around us how great it is to know you. Amen.

Stars in the Sky

Abram's wife, Sarai, could not have children, but God promised that their family would become so big, it would be like the stars in the sky. Abram believed God's impossible, unbreakable promise.

"God said, 'Look at the sky. There are so many stars you cannot count them. And your descendants will be too many to count.'

Abram believed the Lord. And the Lord accepted Abram's faith, and that faith made him right with God." (Genesis 15:5-6)

Dear God,
I know that you are super-powerful and that you are always good. You can keep promises that would be impossible for anyone else to keep. **Wow!**
Thank you that none of your promises can ever be broken.
Please help me to be like Abram and believe in your promises to me, even when they seem impossible.
Amen.

A Baby at Last

When Abraham and Sarah were nearly 100 years old, God gave them a son. They called him Isaac. They laughed with happiness that God had kept his impossible promise.

"Abraham was 100 years old when his son Isaac was born. And Sarah said, 'God has made me laugh. Everyone who hears about this will laugh with me.'" (Genesis 21:5-6)

Dear God,
You gave Abraham and Sarah a son even though it was impossible. **Wow!**
Thank you that we can see in this true story that you always keep your promises.
Sometimes things happen that make us feel sad or worried. **Please** remind us that you are always keeping all of your promises. As we think about that, **please** give us the same happiness that you gave Abraham and Sarah.
Amen.

Jacob's Sneaky Trick

Jacob tricked his dad, Isaac, into giving God's promises to Jacob instead of to his older brother, Esau. But this was all part of God's good plan.

"God told Rebekah, 'The older will serve the younger.' … God said this before they were born so that the one chosen would be chosen because of God's own plan."

(Romans 9:11-12)

Dear God,
Thank you that your plans always happen. **Thank you** that even though Jacob was wrong to lie and trick, you still made sure things happened just as you wanted them to.
Sorry that sometimes I am like Jacob and I take what I want even if it makes other people lose out.
When I am like Jacob and I don't obey you, **please** remind me that your plans will still happen and that I can still be part of them.
Amen.

Jacob's Special Dream

God gave Jacob a dream. Jacob saw a stairway between earth and heaven. God promised Jacob a huge family who had a good land to live in. God promised to use Jacob's family to bring happiness to people all over the earth as they lived under God's rule.

"Jacob dreamed that there was a ladder resting on the earth and reaching up into heaven. And he saw angels of God going up and coming down the ladder. And then Jacob saw the Lord standing above the ladder." (Genesis 28:12-13)

Dear God,
You are in heaven and you rule heaven and earth. **Wow!** You have promised that if we love King Jesus, one day we will live with you in heaven. **Wow!**
Please remind us every day that you are in heaven and that you are ruling everything, everywhere.
Please remind us that everything that happens in our day is part of your good plan.
Amen.

Joseph in Trouble

Joseph's brothers really did not like him, so they sold him to be a slave. Then Joseph was put in prison. But he knew that God was with him and that God had a plan.

"The Lord was with Joseph and showed him kindness."

(Genesis 39:21)

Dear God,
Sometimes things happen that I do not like.
Sometimes people say things or do things that make me feel sad or scared.
Thank you that you are with me when these things happen. I am never on my own.
When I feel lonely, sad or scared, **please** help me to trust you and to ask you for help.
Amen.

14 Joseph and the King of Egypt

God made it so that Joseph could understand the king of Egypt's dreams and explain what they meant. So the king took Joseph out of prison and put him in charge of the whole of Egypt.

"The king said to Joseph, 'God has shown you all this. There is no one as wise and understanding as you are.'" (Genesis 41:39)

Dear God,
We praise you because you know everything. **Wow!** We **thank you** that you explain great truths to us today in the Bible.
Thank you that you looked after Joseph when things were hard for him and when things went well for him.
Thank you that you are always looking after us, too, wherever we are, however we are feeling, and whatever we are doing.
Amen.

Joseph Meets His Brothers

Joseph's brothers had sold Joseph as a slave. When they met Joseph years later, Joseph was kind to them. He told his brothers that God had used everything to keep his promise to look after their family.

"God turned your evil into good. It was to save the lives of many people." (Genesis 50:20)

Dear God,
I praise you that you are so powerful that nothing can stop you keeping your promises — not even people's mistakes or meanness. **Wow!**
Thank you that when I do not love and obey you, I can say **sorry** and you will forgive me.
Please help me to be kind to people who are mean to me, just like Joseph was kind to his brothers, and just like you are kind to me.
Amen.

A Baby in the River

The king of Egypt made God's people slaves. One Israelite mother kept her baby safe by putting him in a basket on the River Nile. The king's daughter found him and looked after him. She called him Moses.

"The king's daughter named him Moses, because she had pulled him out of the water." (Exodus 2:10)

Dear God,
Sometimes things happen to us that make us feel sad.
Sometimes people in this world are mean to others.
Thank you that even when life is hard, you are at work.
Thank you that you looked after Moses, so that he could grow up to lead your people.
We know that you have good plans for us, too.
When I feel sad or someone has been mean, **please** remind me that no one and nothing can stop your promises coming true. Amen.

Moses and the Burning Bush

Moses saw a fire that didn't burn anything up. A voice spoke from the fire. It was God! God promised that he would use Moses to free the Israelites from Egypt and take them to a good land.

"Moses saw that the bush was on fire, but it was not burning up. So Moses said, 'I will go closer to this strange thing. How can a bush continue burning without burning up?'" (Exodus 3:2-3)

Dear God,
You can appear as a fire and speak from the flames. **Wow!** **Thank you** that you are so much more powerful than us, and so different to us.
Thank you that we get to listen to you speak to us in the Bible, just as Moses listened to you speak from the fire.
Please keep teaching us more and more about how amazing you are, and more and more about how amazing your promises are.
Amen.

Let My People Go!

God sent plagues to Egypt to show the king that God is more powerful, and to make the king let God's people go free. But the king kept saying "NO!"

"The king of Egypt said, 'Who is the Lord? Why should I obey him and let Israel go? I do not know the Lord. And I will not let Israel go.'"

(Exodus 5:2)

Dear God,

It is sad that, just like the king of Egypt, lots of people do not think you are in charge and they do not care about obeying you.

Please be at work in the hearts of the people we know who don't treat you as God. Show them that you are real, and powerful, and good.

And **please** be at work in our hearts, too, so that we say YES every day to living with you as our loving king. Amen.

The Rescue from Egypt

God told his people to put the blood of a lamb around their doors so that none of them would die in the last plague. God kept those people safe. The king of Egypt let God's people go free.

God said, "The blood will be a sign on the houses where you are. When I see the blood, I will pass over you. Nothing terrible will hurt you when I punish the land of Egypt."

(Exodus 12:13)

Dear God,

Thank you that you gave your people a way to be rescued from your judgment of Egypt.

Thank you that trusting in the lamb's blood kept them safe.

Thank you that you give us a way to be rescued from your judgment of everyone.

You sent Jesus to be like a lamb.

Thank you that his blood can keep us safe, because he died so that we can be forgiven for the ways we don't love and obey you. What an amazing rescue. **Wow!** Amen.

A Path through the Sea

The king of Egypt chased God's people. He wanted to make them his slaves again. So God parted the Red Sea and his people walked through it to the other side. They were safe!

"The Israelites went through the sea on dry land. A wall of water was on both sides." (Exodus 14:22)

Dear God,
You pushed a whole sea into two big walls of water. **Wow!**
You used all of your power to keep your people safe. **Thank you** that today, you use all of your power to look after us!
There is no one else like you, God. No one else can do what you do. You are the greatest king. **Wow!**
Amen.

God's Commands

At Mount Sinai, God met with Moses. God told Moses that he had rescued the Israelites to be his special family. He showed the people how to obey him by giving them Ten Commandments.

God said, "I am the Lord your God. I brought you out of the land of Egypt where you were slaves. You must not have any other gods except me."

(Exodus 20:2-3)

Dear God,
Thank you for telling us how to live in your world.
Your commands are good!
Please give me strength to obey you, even when it is hard.
Please help me worship you, respect you, and love you.
Please help me to obey my parents and love other people, just as you command.
And **thank you** that, when I don't obey you, you are always ready to forgive me.
Amen.

God's Tent

On their way to the good land God had promised them, God's people lived in tents in the wilderness. God came to live among his people in a special tent. It was called the tabernacle.

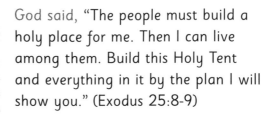

God said, "The people must build a holy place for me. Then I can live among them. Build this Holy Tent and everything in it by the plan I will show you." (Exodus 25:8-9)

Dear God,
You dwelled in the tabernacle when your people lived in the wilderness. **Wow!** Dear Jesus, you are God, and you came and lived in this world as a man. **Wow wow!**
Dear Holy Spirit, you have come to live in all of Jesus's followers today. **Wow wow wow!**
Dear God, one day all your people will enjoy living with you forever. **Wow wow wow wow!**
Please keep reminding me that you are with me – that you are closer than close to me. **Thank you** that I never need to feel lonely. Amen.

Making a Not-God

The Israelites made a not-god. It was a calf, made from gold. They worshipped the not-god instead of the real God. God was angry, but he chose to forgive his people. Moses took the not-god apart.

"The Lord said ... 'The people ... have done a terrible sin. They have quickly turned away from the things I commanded them to do. They have made for themselves a calf of melted gold. They have worshiped that calf.'" (Exodus 32:7-8)

Dear God,
It is sad that even though you had made them and rescued them, the people chose to love something else more than they loved you. We are **sorry** that sometimes we also love things more than we love you.
We are **sorry** that sometimes we act like other things are more important than you, even though you made us and you rescued us. **Please** forgive us, just like you forgave your people in the wilderness. **Please** cause us to worship you, and not to worship anything else.
Amen.

Joshua, Caleb, and the Explorers

God's people reached the good land God had promised to give them. But they were so scared of the people who lived there that they forgot God's promise, and so they would not go into it. Only Joshua and Caleb trusted God – so only Joshua and Caleb were allowed into the land.

Joshua and Caleb said about God, "He will give us that land where much food grows. Don't turn against the Lord! Don't be afraid of the people in that land!" (Numbers 14:8-9)

Dear God,
We are **sorry** that sometimes we forget that you always keep all your promises.
We are **sorry** that sometimes we are too scared of other people to obey you.
Please forgive us.
Give us hearts that are like Joshua and Caleb's were, so that we are sure you really will always keep all of your promises. **Please** make us brave and obedient.
Amen.

Moses Sees the Land

Moses had led God's people out of Egypt.
Before Moses died, God let him see the good land
that God had promised to give his people.

"Then the Lord said to Moses, 'This is the land I promised to Abraham, Isaac and Jacob. I said to them, "I will give this land to your descendants." I have let you look at it, Moses.'" (Deuteronomy 34:4)

Dear God,
Thank you that you worked through Moses to lead your people to the promised land.
Thank you that you are working in our lives to lead us to the best land — to your forever place in the life after this one.
Thank you that after we die we will get to enjoy living there, forever.
Please keep us following our leader, the Lord Jesus, till we live in the best land of all. Amen.

Rahab and the Explorers

Rahab lived in Jericho. She knew that God is the real God who rescued his people from Egypt. So when two explorers from God's people came to Jericho, she hid them from the king and kept them safe.

Rahab said, "We have heard how the Lord helped you. We heard how he dried up the Red Sea..."

(Joshua 2:10)

Dear God,
Thank you that anyone can be part of your people, whoever they are and wherever they live.
Rahab was right. You are the real God. You do rescue your people. **Wow!**
Thank you that, like Rahab, I can be part of your people just by asking you.
Amen.

The Walls of Jericho

God told the Israelites to march round the big, big walls of Jericho for six days, and then, on the seventh day, to march round again, blow their trumpets, and shout. When they did, God made the walls fall down!

"It was by faith that the walls of Jericho fell. They fell after the people had marched around the walls of Jericho for seven days."

(Hebrews 11:30)

Dear God,
You are so powerful that you can make big, big walls fall down. **Wow!**
You are so powerful that you can keep any promise that you make — even when it sounds impossible to us. **Wow!**
Please help me believe what you say, just like the Israelites did.
Please help me to trust you and obey what you tell me to do, because I know you will always keep all of your promises. Amen.

Joshua Says Goodbye

Before he died, Joshua reminded the people that God had kept all his promises and given them a good land to live in. He told the people they needed to choose whether to love and obey God or not.

Joshua said, "As for me and my family, we will serve the Lord."

(Joshua 24:15)

Dear God,

Thank you that Joshua's life shows us that you always keep your promises.

Thank you that you have promised to love us, and to forgive us when we ask you to, and to take us to live with you in the life after this one.

We love you. And we want to obey you, even when we find that hard to do.

Please help us choose to serve you, Lord.

Amen.

Deborah, Barak, and the Big Battle

God's people worshipped not-gods. God let their enemies, led by Sisera, defeat them. But God gave his people a leader, Deborah. She told them how to obey God. And God gave his people victory over their enemies.

Deborah said, "Today is the day the Lord will help you defeat Sisera. You know the Lord has already cleared the way for you." (Judges 4:14)

Dear God,

Thank you that you never give up on your people – even when we love other things more than we love you.
Thank you for sending Jesus to tell us how to obey you.
Thank you for sending Jesus to win victory over sin and death. **Thank you** that you have cleared the way for us to enjoy living with you forever.
Thank you that we are your people, and that you will never, ever give up on us.
Amen.

Samson Saves the Israelites

God made Samson very, very strong. The Philistines were the enemies of God's people and they made him a prisoner. But Samson pushed the pillars of a building over. He died, but so did the Philistines.

"Samson said, 'Let me die with these Philistines!' Then he pushed as hard as he could. And the temple fell on the kings and all the people in it."

(Judges 16:30)

Dear God,
You worked through Samson's death to save your people from their enemies. **Wow!**
You worked through Jesus's death to save us from our enemies! **Wow!**
Thank you that when Jesus died, he defeated death so that we can live with you forever.
Thank you that I never need to be scared, even when I feel weak, because Jesus is my strength and my rescuer. Amen.

Ruth Finds a Family

Ruth was not part of God's people, but she chose to love and obey God. She became one of his people. Boaz protected her and gave her food. They ended up getting married and having a son, Obed.

Boaz said to Ruth, "May you be richly rewarded by the Lord, the God of Israel, under whose wings you have come to take refuge."

(Ruth 2:12, NIV)

Dear God,
Thank you that anyone can become part of your people by choosing to love and obey you.
Thank you that you work through your people to look after your people.
Please make me brave like Ruth, choosing to love and obey you even when it is hard.
Please make me kind like Boaz, choosing to look after and protect people who need my help.
Amen.

Hannah's Special Son

Hannah was sad and prayed to God. She asked God for a baby. God heard her and helped her, and she had a baby.

"Hannah said, 'The Lord has filled my heart with joy ... I am glad because you have helped me.'"

(1 Samuel 2:1)

Dear God,
Thank you that you heard Hannah's prayers and gave her a baby.
Thank you that you hear my prayers and help me.
Thank you that you give happiness to your people.
Please help me to remember that I can talk to you about anything that makes me feel happy and anything that makes me feel sad.
Amen.

We Want a King!

God's people wanted a king like the other nations had, instead of having God as their king. God let them have a king, called Saul. Saul was big and strong, but he did not always love and obey God.

The people said, "We want a king to rule over us. Then we will be the same as all the other nations."

(1 Samuel 8:19-20)

Dear God,
It is sad when people choose to have a king who is not you. It is sad when people choose to be just like everybody else, instead of being like you.
I am **sorry** that sometimes I want to be just like other people too. Sometimes I don't love you or obey you as my king.
Thank you that you forgive me.
Please help me to care more about loving and obeying you than I do about growing big or strong or clever or pretty or anything else. Amen.

God Chooses a King

God gave his people the king they needed. He sent his messenger Samuel to Jesse's family. God told Samuel to choose the youngest son, David, to be the next king.

"People look at the outside of a person, but the Lord looks at the heart." (1 Samuel 16:7)

Dear God,
Thank you that you chose David to be your king because his heart loved you and wanted to obey you.
Thank you that you sent King Jesus to be our king.
Thank you that Jesus's heart always loves and obeys you.
Please remind me that you care most about what someone is like on the inside, and that how tall or good-looking or strong we are does not matter anywhere near as much.
Please give me a heart that loves and obeys you.
Amen.

David and Goliath

God's people faced a huge enemy, Goliath. They could not beat him. But God's king, David, rescued them by killing Goliath with his sling and his stones.

"David said to [Goliath], 'You come to me using a sword, a large spear and a small spear. But I come to you in the name of the Lord of heaven's armies.'" (1 Samuel 17:45)

Dear God,
You can use anyone to do anything. **Wow!**
Thank you that you made King David able to beat Goliath, the enemy of your people, so that they could live in peace.
Thank you that you made King Jesus able to beat death, our greatest enemy, so that we can live with you forever.
King Jesus, you love to help me. You are always on my side! **Wow!**
Amen.

A King Forever

David was a great king of God's people. God promised him that one day an even greater king of God's people would come from David's family. This king would rule forever.

"God has given us a powerful Savior from the family of God's servant David." (Luke 1:69)

Dear God,
You are great. There is no one else like you. **Wow!**
Thank you for keeping your promise to David.
Thank you for giving your people a perfect forever king – Jesus.
We have a king who always knows what is right and who always does what is right. **Wow!**
Thank you, God, for King Jesus.
Amen.

King Solomon

God gave King Solomon wisdom, and God's people were happy. But then Solomon stopped being wise and decided to worship not-gods. God was not happy.

"Solomon did what the Lord said was wrong. He did not follow the Lord completely as his father David had done." (1 Kings 11:6)

Dear Jesus,
Thank you that you are our perfect king. You always know what is right and you always do what is right. Sometimes, we don't know what to do. **Please** help us to listen to you and **please** guide us by your Spirit. Sometimes, we don't love and obey you. **Please** forgive us and **please** enable us to love you more and love not-gods less.
Amen.

Things Go Very Wrong

God's people stopped loving and obeying God. They worshipped not-gods instead. God sent messengers to tell them to believe him, obey him, and say sorry to him, so they could be forgiven by him. But they didn't listen.

"My people ask wooden idols for advice ... They have chased after other gods. They have left their own God." (Hosea 4:12)

Dear God,

Lots of people choose not to love and obey you. We are **sorry** that sometimes we are those people – that sometimes, we do not love and obey you.

Thank you that you love people even when they don't love you, and that anyone who is sorry can be forgiven.

Thank you that you speak to us in your word, the Bible, to remind us to believe your promises, obey your commands, and ask for your forgiveness.

We want to love and obey you, God. **Please** help us to do so. Amen.

Elijah and the Fire

Elijah was God's messenger. God proved to the people that he was the real God, and that Elijah was his messenger, by sending fire from heaven to set a dead bull on fire. The people realized that God is the real God.

"If the Lord is the true God, follow him." (1 Kings 18:21)

Dear God,
You are the real God, the only God. **Wow!**
Thank you that you sent Elijah as your messenger.
Thank you that you sent fire to prove that you are real.
Thank you that you sent Jesus as your greatest messenger. **Thank you** that you raised him from the dead to show that you are real.
We know that you are the true God. We want to follow you. **Please** help us to love you, listen to you, and obey you. Amen.

A King is Coming

Isaiah was God's messenger. Isaiah warned the people that because they did not love and obey God, they would not be able to live in his good land. But he also promised the people that one day God would send his special king, who would rescue them and rule them forever.

"God will give a son to us.
   He will be responsible for leading
   the people.
His name will be Wonderful
Counselor, Powerful God,
   Father Who Lives Forever,
   Prince of Peace." (Isaiah 9:6)

Dear Jesus,
Thank you that you are God's promised king, and that you were born at the first Christmas to rescue us and rule us forever.
You always know what is best for us. **Wow!**
You are super-powerful and can do anything. **Wow!**
You live forever, and you can give us life forever too. **Wow!**
You give us peace with God and you help us make peace with others. **Wow!**
Thank you that you are my king, Jesus. Amen.

Jonah and the Big Fish

Jonah did not want to obey God's command to tell the people of Nineveh about God, so he ran away. God sent a storm to stop him and then a big fish to swallow him. The fish kept Jonah safe, and then he went and told the people of Nineveh about God.

"The Lord caused a very big fish to swallow Jonah. Jonah was in the stomach of the fish three days and three nights." (Jonah 1:17)

Dear God,
You are in charge of the weather and of every fish in the sea. **Wow!**
You rescued Jonah even though he had disobeyed you. **Wow!**
I know that I do not always obey you. Sometimes I am grumpy. Sometimes I am whiny. Sometimes I am angry. Sometimes I do what I want to do, instead of doing what is kind to others. But you still love me and forgive me. **Wow!**
Amen.

Out of the Land

God's people kept disobeying him, so he made them leave the good land he'd given them. But he promised to bring them back, to give them his special king, and to send his Spirit to live in them.

"I will put my Spirit inside you. And I will help you live by my rules … You will be my people, and I will be your God." (Ezekiel 36:27-28)

Dear God,
You have kept your promises that you made all those years ago. **Wow!**
You have sent your special forever king, Jesus. **Wow!**
You have given us a place in your forever land in the life after this one. **Wow!**
You have given us your Spirit to live in us and help us obey you. **Wow!**
Thank you for keeping your promises to us, God. We love you. Amen.

Daniel in the Lions' Den

Daniel prayed to God even when the king of Babylon told him not to. So Daniel was thrown into a den of lions. God sent an angel to keep Daniel safe. The king told everyone that God is the greatest ruler, and that he can rescue people.

The king said, "God rescues and saves people.
God does mighty miracles in heaven and on earth.
God saved Daniel from the power of the lions."

(Daniel 6:27)

Dear God,
You are more powerful than any lion. You are the greatest ruler, and you rescue people. **Wow!**
Thank you that you rescued Daniel from the lions.
Thank you that you rescue us from sin and death.
Thank you that Daniel could enjoy life after the lions' den. **Thank you** that we can enjoy life with you after we die.
When I am scared, **please** remind me to trust you and talk to you. Amen.

The Brave Queen

Queen Esther of Persia was one of God's people. A man named Haman made a nasty plan to get rid of all God's people. Esther risked her life to speak to the king when she wasn't allowed. She told him about the plan, and the king stopped it. Because Esther was brave, God's people were safe!

"You may have been chosen queen for just such a time as this."

(Esther 4:14)

Dear God,
You put Esther in just the right place at just the right time. **Wow!**
You made Esther brave so that she could do the right thing. **Wow!**
I know that you have put me in just the place you want me to be.
Thank you that I can help your people.
Thank you that I can tell people about you.
Please make me brave so that I will do what you want me to do. Amen.

Back in the Land Again

God's people came back to the land he had promised to give them. They rebuilt their city and its wall. God told them that one day, the person who would keep all his promises would arrive.

"The Lord of heaven's armies says, 'I will send my messenger. He will prepare the way for me to come. Suddenly, the Lord you are looking for will come to his Temple.'"

(Malachi 3:1)

Dear God,
Thank you that you always keep all your promises.
Thank you that the person who makes all your promises come true has arrived. I know that his name is Jesus.
Thank you that I can look forward to the day when Jesus comes back to this world, and I get to enjoy life with you forever.
On days when things go wrong, **please** remind me that one day Jesus will come back and put everything right.
Amen.

An Angel Visits Mary

God sent the angel Gabriel to tell Mary that she was going to have a baby. He would be called Jesus. He would be God's Son, he would be the king of God's people, and he would rule forever.

The angel said to Mary, "You will give birth to a son, and you will name him Jesus. He will be great, and people will call him the Son of the Most High." (Luke 1:31-32)

Dear God,
Thank you for sending your Son to this world, just as you promised to.
Thank you that Jesus grew as a baby inside Mary, just as I grew as a baby inside my mother.
Thank you that in lots of ways, Jesus is just like me.
Thank you that in lots of other ways, he is much, much, much more special than me!
Amen.

The Angel Speaks to Joseph

God sent the angel Gabriel to tell Joseph to marry Mary. Gabriel said that God's Holy Spirit had put the baby inside her. The angel told Joseph to call the baby Jesus, which means "God saves." Joseph believed God's angel, so he did what the angel had said.

The angel said to Joseph, "You will name the son Jesus. Give him that name because he will save his people from their sins." (Matthew 1:21)

Dear Jesus,

Thank you that you came to save us from our sins, so that we could enjoy living with you as our king forever. We know that we sin. We are **sorry** that we do not always love and obey you as we should.

Thank you that you save anyone who asks you to forgive them.

Every time I hear the name "Jesus," **please** remind me that you are the way that God saves people.

Amen.

Mary's Thank-You Song

Mary went to visit her relative Elizabeth. She was too old to have children, but God had given her a baby anyway. Elizabeth told Mary that God was keeping all his promises. Mary was so happy and amazed that she sang a thank-you song to God.

"My soul praises the Lord; my heart is happy because God is my Savior." (Luke 1:46-47)

God, you are amazing! I am so happy, because you are my rescuer and you care for me. **Wow!**
I'm not special or strong, but I'm part of your story. **Wow!**
You are good to everyone who knows that you are God. **Wow!**
You are kind to everyone who knows that they need you. **Wow!**
You are keeping all the promises you have made. Wow!
I love you, God. Amen.

Jesus is Born

Mary and Joseph went to Bethlehem. Jesus was born there. That night, an angel appeared to some shepherds nearby. He told them that a baby had just been born, and that he was God's promise-keeping king, who would rescue them. The shepherds rushed to see Jesus.

"Then the shepherds went back to their sheep, praising God and thanking him for everything that they had seen and heard. It was just as the angel had told them."

(Luke 2:20)

Dear God,

We praise you that Jesus is the way that you keep all of your promises. **Wow!**

We praise you that he is our rescuer and our king. **Wow!**

Thank you for sending the angel to tell the shepherds about Jesus.

Thank you for the people who tell me about Jesus. Please keep me believing the truth about Jesus.

Amen.

50 Simeon and Anna Meet Jesus

Simeon and Anna were old. They had been waiting for years and years to see God's king. When they met the baby Jesus, they were very excited. They knew he was the way God would bring joy to people all over the world.

Simeon said, "I have seen your Salvation with my own eyes."

(Luke 2:30)

Dear God,
Thank you that anyone can know that Jesus loves them and forgives them.
Thank you that Jesus brings joy to all kinds of people all over the world.
Jesus is amazing! **Thank you** that even though I can't see him with my eyes like Simeon and Anna did, I can know Jesus as my king and my friend in my heart.
Please keep me excited about knowing Jesus.
Amen.

Wise Men Arrive

God put a new star in the sky for some wise men to follow to find God's promise-keeping king. When they reached Bethlehem, the wise men bowed down to Jesus and gave him the best presents they had.

"They bowed down and worshiped the child. They opened the gifts they brought for him. They gave him treasures of gold, frankincense, and myrrh." (Matthew 2:11)

Dear Jesus,
Wise people treat you as their king.
You are so amazing that you are worth giving everything to, just like those wise men did.
Thank you that I don't have to travel a long way to find you.
Thank you that you are right here with me, by your Spirit.
I can love and worship you, right where I am.
Please show me how! Amen.

Jesus Escapes

King Herod did not want Jesus to be the king. He did not want Jesus to stay alive. But God sent an angel to tell Joseph to take Mary and Jesus to Egypt, where they were safe.

"An angel of the Lord came to Joseph in a dream. The angel said, 'Get up! Take the child and his mother and escape to Egypt.'"

(Matthew 2:13)

Dear God,
It is sad that there are lots of countries where the leaders really do not like Jesus. They make it very, very hard to live as your people.
But we **thank you** that no one and nothing can stop Jesus being the king. Even Herod couldn't stop your plans for Jesus!
Please keep giving faith, bravery, and joy to your people, especially those who live in places where it is dangerous to love and obey Jesus. Amen.

The Baptism of Jesus

John the Baptist told people to get ready for God to arrive. When John baptized Jesus, God's Spirit came to Jesus, looking like a dove. And God the Father spoke about Jesus from heaven.

"Jesus was baptized and came up out of the water ... And a voice spoke from heaven. The voice said, 'This is my Son and I love him. I am very pleased with him.'"

(Matthew 3:16-17)

Dear Jesus,
We know that your Father loves you completely. **Wow!** We know that because you are perfect, your Father is totally pleased with you. **Wow!**
Jesus, **thank you** that if we are following you then your Father feels the same way about us as he does about you. We are loved completely by God!
Please keep helping our hearts to say **"Wow"** about that.
Amen.

Jesus in the Desert

While he was on his own in the desert, Jesus was tempted three times by the devil to disobey God. Each time, Jesus said "no" and obeyed God. The devil's plan had not worked. Jesus had obeyed his Father perfectly.

"Jesus said to the devil, 'Go away from me, Satan! It is written in the Scriptures, "You must worship the Lord your God. Serve only him!"'"

(Matthew 4:10)

Dear Jesus,
You always loved your Father, so you always said "no" to the devil when he tempted you to disobey God. **Wow!** Lord Jesus, sometimes I am tempted to think or say or do something that is wrong. When this happens, **please** work in me by your Spirit to strengthen me to say "no" and to choose to love God instead, just like you did. And when I do disobey God, **please** remind me that because you always obeyed, I can always be forgiven. Amen.

Jesus Chooses His Friends

Jesus chose twelve men to be his special friends. He started sharing his good-news message: that because he had arrived, people could be part of God's kingdom. He told everyone to love and obey him as their king and to believe that he was making all God's promises come true.

"'The time has come,' [Jesus] said. 'The kingdom of God has come near. Repent and believe the good news!'" (Mark 1:15, NIV)

Dear King Jesus,
Because you came to this world, anyone can be part of your kingdom. **Wow!**
Thank you that you invite all people to follow you as your friends – including me!
Please help me to believe that you are the way that all God's promises come true, and to choose to love and obey you as my king.
Amen.

Get Up!

Some men had a friend whose legs didn't work. They wanted him to get to Jesus, so they lowered him through a hole in a roof. Jesus told the man that his sins were forgiven. Then, to show he was powerful enough to forgive his sins, Jesus fixed the man's legs, too!

Jesus said, "'I will prove to you that the Son of Man has authority on earth to forgive sins.' So Jesus said to the paralyzed man, 'I tell you, stand up. Take your mat and go home.'" (Mark 2:10-11)

Dear Jesus,
You are so powerful that you can do anything. **Wow!** We know that what we most need is not a body that works, but to be forgiven for the ways that we have not loved and obeyed you.
So, **please** forgive me for my sins. And **please** look after my body, too.
When I am sick or I feel sad, **please** remind me that you have forgiven me and I am your friend. I know you love me very much! Amen.

A Dead Man Lives!

Jesus saw a woman whose son had died. Jesus felt so sad deep down inside that his tummy hurt. Jesus told the man who had died to get up... and he did! He had come back to life!

"Jesus said, 'Young man, I tell you, get up!' The son sat up and began to talk." (Luke 7:14-15)

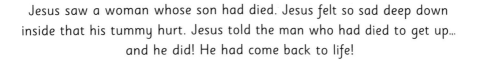

Dear Jesus,
Thank you that you care about things that make me sad.
Thank you that you have the power to change things that make me sad.
Thank you that you can give people life after they have died. That is amazing!
When I feel sad about something going wrong, **please** remind me that you care about me.
And **please** remind me that one day your friends will live with you forever, where nothing ever goes wrong. Amen.

58 ⟩ John the Baptist's Question

John the Baptist wondered if Jesus really was God's promise-keeping king. Jesus reminded John that he was making blind people see, fixing lame people's legs, bringing dead people back to life, and telling people the good news that God had come to rescue them.

"John the Baptist sent us to you with this question: 'Are you the One who is coming, or should we wait for another?'" (Luke 7:20)

Dear King Jesus,
Thank you that you like it when we ask you questions and think hard about who you are. **Thank you** that you showed us who you really are by all the things you did. You can make broken things work again, dead people live again, and sinners become friends with you again. **Wow!** One day your friends will live in your perfect world, where nothing breaks and no one dies.
Please make our hearts very excited about being there with you! Amen.

Jesus and the Storm

Jesus was crossing a sea on a boat with his friends. A huge storm started and the disciples thought they would sink. "Quiet! Be still!" Jesus told the storm. And... it was! Jesus told his friends that they did not need to be scared. They just needed to believe in him.

"Jesus stood up and commanded the wind and the waves to stop. He said, 'Quiet! Be still!' Then the wind stopped, and the lake became calm." (Mark 4:39)

Lord Jesus,
You are so in charge of everything that you can even tell the wind and the waves what to do. **Wow!**
Thank you that I get to be your friend.
Jesus, if you can calm a storm, you can definitely help me!
Sometimes I feel scared. **Thank you** that when I feel that way, you are with me, and you can help me, and you love me. **Please** help me to trust you whenever I am frightened. Amen.

Come Out of Him!

Jesus met a man who felt mixed up and very miserable because some evil spirits had made him feel that way. Jesus told the spirits to come out of the man. They did, and the man was completely changed. He went and told everyone he met that Jesus had helped him.

"Jesus sent [the man he had helped] away, saying, 'Go back home and tell people what God did for you.' So the man went all over town telling how much Jesus had done for him." (Luke 8:38-39)

Dear Jesus,
Thank you that nothing is too hard for you to do.
Thank you that nothing is too broken for you to fix.
I don't need to be scared of anything if I am your friend!
Thank you that everyone I know can be friends with you.
Please use me to tell other people about how great you are and how much you have done for me.
Amen.

Jesus Raises a Dead Girl to Life

Jesus was going to Jairus' house to see his very sick daughter. But before he got there, she died. "Don't be afraid. Just believe," Jesus said to Jairus. Jesus went into the room where the dead girl was. He told her to stand up. And she did! Everyone was amazed!

"[Jesus] took hold of the girl's hand and said to her, 'Talitha, koum!' (This means, 'Little girl, I tell you to stand up!') The girl stood right up and began walking."

(Mark 5:41-42)

Dear Jesus,
You are good and you are powerful. **Wow!**
You can do things that no one else can do. You can raise someone from the dead as easily as we can wake someone up from being asleep. **Wow!**
Thank you that you can give us life after we die, in the life after this one.
Thank you that we do not need to be worried about dying, or anything else.
Amen.

Buried Treasure

Jesus used stories called parables to tell truths about him and his kingdom. In one parable, he said his kingdom is like treasure buried in a field. When a man found it, he sold everything he had so that he could buy the field and enjoy the treasure. He was so happy!

Jesus said, "The kingdom of heaven is like a treasure hidden in a field. One day a man found the treasure … The man was very happy to find the treasure. He went and sold everything that he owned to buy that field."

(Matthew 13:44)

Dear King Jesus,
Thank you for all the good things you have given me.
Thank you for toys and teddies and friends and food.
Thank you that the very best thing you can give is a place in your kingdom. It is wonderful to be loved by you and to be looked after by you!
Whenever I am enjoying something good, **please** remind me that being part of your kingdom is the very best thing. Amen.

Jesus Feeds the Crowds

Jesus took five loaves of bread and two fish. He fed thousands and thousands of people till they were full. Then Jesus explained that he is the "bread of life," who can give us life with God forever.

Jesus said, "He who believes has eternal life. I am the bread that gives life." (John 6:47-48)

Dear Jesus,
Thank you for giving me the food I ate today. **Thank you** that food keeps me alive.
Thank you, Jesus, that you are the bread of life.
Thank you that you can give me forever life.
Next time I eat some bread, **please** help me remember that eating bread gives me life today, but that believing in you gives me life forever – eternal life.
Amen.

Who Do You Say I Am?

People had lots of ideas about who they thought Jesus was –
a messenger from God, a teacher, and so on. Jesus's friend Simon
Peter knew who Jesus was – the king who God had promised to send,
the Son of God.

"Jesus asked them, 'And who do you say I am?' Simon Peter answered, 'You are the Christ, the Son of the living God.'" (Matthew 16:15-16)

Dear God,
Thank you for showing Peter who Jesus is.
Thank you that you can show me who Jesus is.
Please make me more and more sure that Jesus is your promised king, the Christ; and that Jesus is your Son.
Thank you that, just like Peter, I can be friends with King Jesus.
Amen.

Jesus on the Mountain

Jesus and three of his friends went up a mountain. Jesus looked very different – his face shone and his clothes became bright. God the Father spoke to Jesus's friends and told them that Jesus is his Son who people need to listen to.

"This is my Son, whom I love; with him I am well pleased. Listen to him!" (Matthew 17:5, NIV)

Dear God,
Thank you for telling us that Jesus is your Son. We are amazed that Jesus only ever thought, said, and did things that made you very pleased. **Wow!**
Please enable us to love Jesus, to listen to Jesus, and to do what he says.
Thank you that Jesus says that when we don't obey him, we can ask for forgiveness, and you will always say "yes."
Amen.

The Good Samaritan

Jesus told a story about a man who was attacked by robbers. Two men just walked past where he lay. A third man came. He was not friends with the man who was lying there. He was not from the same country. But he helped him. Jesus told people to be kind like the third man was.

Jesus said, "Which one of these three men do you think was a neighbor to the man who was attacked by the robbers? ... Go and do the same thing he did!" (Luke 10:36-37)

Dear Jesus,
Thank you that you showed your love for God by loving others.
Jesus, I love you. So I want to love others too.
Please be at work in me so that I can be kind to people who I am not friends with, and so that I can be kind even to people who have been mean to me.
Please show me how I can love the people I spend time with this week.
Make me more like you, Jesus! Amen.

Jesus Teaches His Friends How to Pray

Jesus taught his friends how to talk to God like he did. Jesus told his friends that anyone who lives with him as their king can call God their Father. And they can know that God gives them his Holy Spirit.

"Pray and ask God for everything you need. And when you pray, always give thanks."

(Philippians 4:6)

Our Father in heaven, you are the greatest!
Please make your kingdom grow.
Please cause your plans to happen on earth, just as they do in heaven.
Please give us what you know we need today.
Please forgive us for the ways we have not loved you and not loved other people.
We will forgive people who are unkind to us.
Please help us obey you when we feel like doing what is wrong. Amen.

The Good Shepherd

Jesus said that he is like a shepherd and his people are like sheep. He cares for his people. He came to find his people and make them safe. He loves his people so much that he came to die for them. Jesus is the good shepherd.

"The good shepherd gives his life for the sheep ... I am the good shepherd. I know my sheep, and my sheep know me." (John 10:11, 14)

Dear Jesus, my good shepherd,
Thank you that you came to this world to make me one of your sheep.
Thank you that you died so that I can be part of your people and enjoy life with you forever.
Thank you that you love me so much.
Please help me to hear your voice and obey you, and **please** forgive me when I wander away from you.
Please be my good shepherd, today and every day.
Amen.

The Life After This One

Jesus told a story. A poor man, Lazarus, died, and God took him to live with him in the life after this one. A rich man died too. Because he had not loved God or listened to him, he had nothing good in the life after this one. He could not be where Lazarus was.

"He who believes in the Son has eternal life. But he who does not obey the Son will never have that life." (John 3:36)

Dear Lord Jesus,

Please help us remember that what happens after we die matters even more than what happens in this life.

Thank you for warning us that if we do not ask you to forgive us, after we die we will have to be in a place where there is nothing good.

Thank you for promising us that if we do ask you to forgive us then we can enjoy life with you, where everything is good, forever.

So, **please** forgive us, so that we can look forward to that forever life with you. Amen.

The Religious Leader and the Tax Collector

Jesus told a story about a religious leader who thought he was God's friend because he did lots of good things, and a tax collector who knew he wasn't good but asked God to forgive him. Jesus said the tax collector was forgiven, and was God's friend – and the religious leader was not.

"The tax collector stood at a distance. When he prayed, he would not even look up to heaven … He said, 'God, have mercy on me. I am a sinner!'" (Luke 18:13)

Dear God,
Thank you for explaining that we don't get to be your friends by being good, but by being forgiven.
I know that I have not obeyed you. I know that I do not deserve to be your friend. I am **sorry**.
Thank you that all I need to do to be your friend is to ask you for forgiveness.
Please forgive me.
Amen.

Jesus and the Little Children

When Jesus's friends stopped some little children seeing him, he was very unhappy. Jesus said that his kingdom belongs to people who are like little children – who just come and ask him to be their friend and their king.

Jesus said, "Let the little children come to me. Don't stop them. The kingdom of God belongs to people who are like these little children."

(Mark 10:14)

Dear Jesus,
As a child, I often need to ask people to give me things and to help me with things.
Thank you that this helps me understand how to be part of your kingdom. I don't need to do anything. I don't need to be big or strong. I just need to ask you to be my friend and my king.
Thank you that you always love it when I talk to you.
Amen.

Zacchaeus Welcomes Jesus

Zacchaeus was a rich tax collector who climbed a tree to see Jesus. When he found out that Jesus wanted to be his friend, Zacchaeus was really happy, and he gave a lot of his money away.

"Jesus said, 'Salvation has come to this house today. … The Son of Man came to find lost people and save them.'" (Luke 19:9-10)

Dear Jesus,
Thank you that you came to find and rescue people who love things like money, that don't really make us happy.
Thank you that knowing you is better than anything else, and that loving you makes us happier than anything else. Lord Jesus, as I live as your friend, **please** make me a person who loves to share. **Please** help me to give things away instead of grabbing things for myself.
Thank you that you gave your life so that I could be your friend. Amen.

The King on the Donkey

God had promised that when his promise-keeping king came,
he would ride into Jerusalem on a donkey. So that's what Jesus did.
People realized that Jesus was the king who God had promised to send.
They were very happy and very excited.

"God bless the king who comes in
the name of the Lord! There is
peace in heaven and glory to God!"

(Luke 19:38)

Dear Jesus,
You are the king who God promised to send. **Wow!**
You are the king who keeps all of God's promises. **Wow!**
You are the king who brings us happiness. **Wow!**
Thank you that you rode into Jerusalem on a donkey
to help people understand who you are.
Next time I see a donkey or a horse, **please** remind me
that you are God's promise-keeping king.
Amen.

Jesus at the Temple

Jesus was very unhappy that God's temple was being used to make money instead of to pray. So he tipped over the tables of the people who were selling things. The religious leaders were angry. Some children were excited because they knew that Jesus was God's promise-keeping king.

"Jesus was doing wonderful things... Children [were] praising him in the Temple. The children were saying, 'Praise to the Son of David.'"

(Matthew 21:15)

Dear Jesus,
Thank you that you want people to pray.
Thank you that you love to hear big truths coming out of little mouths — mouths like mine.
Please help me to keep using my mouth to talk to you, all through my day, and to tell the truth about you to the people I meet.
Amen.

A New Special Meal

The night before he died, Jesus ate bread and drank wine with his friends. Jesus said the bread was like his body, which would be broken to rescue them. He told his friends that whenever they drank wine they should remember that he had bled on the cross so they could be forgiven.

"Jesus took a cup [and] said ... 'This is my blood which begins the new agreement that God makes with his people. This blood is poured out for many to forgive their sins.'"

(Matthew 26:27-28)

Dear Jesus,
Thank you that you died on the cross to rescue and forgive us.
Thank you that you gave us a helpful way to remember why you died.
Next time I eat some bread, **please** remind me that you died to rescue me. Next time I drink some juice, **please** remind me that you died so that I can be forgiven.
Thank you that one day I will eat and drink with you in the life after this one. That's amazing! Amen.

Praying in a Garden

Jesus was praying in a garden. He felt very, very sad. He asked God to take away the awful things that would happen when he died on the cross. But Jesus also told God that he would do what God wanted him to do. God sent an angel to strengthen Jesus.

"[Jesus] prayed, 'Abba, Father! You can do all things. Let me not have this cup of suffering. But do what you want, not what I want.'"

(Mark 14:36)

Dear Jesus,
Thank you that when I feel sad or scared or hurt, you know just how that feels.
Thank you that even though you were so sad, you spoke to God and you chose to obey God.
Thank you that you loved me so much that you chose to die so that I can be forgiven, even though it was so hard for you.
I love you, Lord Jesus.
Amen.

The King and the Thief

The religious leaders put Jesus on a cross to die. A thief who was dying on a cross next to him knew who Jesus was. He asked Jesus for a place in Jesus's kingdom. Jesus promised the thief that when they had died, they would both be in Jesus's kingdom in the life after this one.

"Jesus said to [the thief], 'Listen! What I say is true: Today you will be with me in paradise!'"

(Luke 23:43)

Dear Jesus,
Thank you that you died so that anyone can live with you in your perfect place in the life after this one.
Thank you that to have a place in paradise, we don't need to do anything except ask.
Like that thief, I know that you are the king.
Please give me a place in your kingdom.
Thank you that I can live with you forever!
Amen.

Jesus is Alive!

Jesus died on a Friday. On the Sunday, some women who were his friends went to his tomb — and he wasn't there! Some angels came and told the women that Jesus had risen back to life, just as Jesus had promised them he would. Then they saw Jesus — alive!

The angels told the women, "You are looking for Jesus, the one who was killed on the cross. But he is not here. He has risen from death as he said he would." (Matthew 28:5-6)

Dear Jesus,
You were dead, and then you came back to life. You are alive right now. **Wow!**
You are more powerful than death. **Wow!**
Everything that you say will happen, does happen. **Wow!**
Thank you that, because you are alive after dying, one day you will give me life after I die.
Thank you that one day I will get to see you, just like those women did.
I'm very happy you're alive! Amen.

The Strange Stranger

Jesus walked along with two of his friends, but they didn't realize it was him till they ate with him. Later, Jesus appeared to some of his other friends and ate with them, too. He showed them that the Bible said that God had promised that his king would die and then rise and rule forever.

"Jesus opened their minds so they could understand the Scriptures. He said to them, 'It is written that the Christ would be killed and rise from death on the third day.'"

(Luke 24:45-46)

Dear Jesus,
Thank you that your Bible tells us how you appeared to your friends lots of times and in lots of ways, so that we can believe that you are alive.
Thank you that your Bible explains lots of times and in lots of ways that you are God's promise-keeping king. You really are the king forever!
Please make my mind be able to understand your Bible, and my heart be excited about you.
Amen.

Thomas Changes His Mind

Thomas was Jesus's friend. He did not believe Jesus was really alive. Then Jesus appeared to him and spoke to him. Now Thomas believed! Jesus told Thomas that, even without seeing him like Thomas had, lots of people would enjoy knowing that Jesus really is alive.

"Thomas said to [Jesus], 'My Lord and my God!'" (John 20:28)

Dear Jesus,
We have not seen you, but we know that lots and lots and lots of people did see you alive after you died. We know that they spoke with you, and touched you, and ate with you.
Thank you that even though our eyes have not seen you, you have shown our hearts who you are.
So we believe that you are living right now, Jesus. You are our king and our God.
Amen.

Jesus Goes to Heaven

Jesus went back to heaven to be with God the Father. He promised to give his friends the Holy Spirit to live in them and to help them tell people all over the world the truth about him. After he went to heaven, two angels told his friends that one day, Jesus would come back.

"While he was blessing them, he was separated from them and carried into heaven. They worshiped him and then went back to the city very happy." (Luke 24:51-52)

Dear Jesus,
I'm happy about the things that have happened today.
I'm happy because you love me.
I'm happy because you are alive, right now, in heaven. **Wow!**
I'm happy because you have sent your Spirit to live in me. **Wow!**
I'm happy that, one day, you will come back to this world. **Wow!**
Thank you, Jesus! Amen.

The Holy Spirit Arrives

The Holy Spirit came to live in Jesus's friends. The Spirit enabled them to tell people about Jesus. Thousands of people decided to start living with Jesus as their king. To show this, they were baptized.

"Repent and be baptized, every one of you, in the name of Jesus Christ for the forgiveness of your sins. And you will receive the gift of the Holy Spirit." (Acts 2:38, NIV)

Dear God,

Thank you that your Spirit lives in everyone who is following Jesus as their king.

Thank you that your Spirit gives all of your people courage and power to talk about Jesus.

Thank you that you work through what we say to bring other people to follow Jesus too.

Holy Spirit, **please** help me tell people that Jesus is the king and that he loves them.

Amen.

The First Church

Jesus' friends loved listening to the truth about Jesus. They loved meeting together. They loved eating together. They loved praying together. They loved sharing their things with each other. More and more people decided they wanted to live with Jesus as their king.

"They spent their time learning the apostles' teaching. And they continued to share, to break bread, and to pray together." (Acts 2:42)

Dear God,
Thank you for my church.
Thank you for the youngest children and the oldest grown-ups. **Thank you** for all the ways we are different.
Thank you that we all love Jesus.
Please help me to listen to people in my church who tell me the truth about Jesus. **Please** show me how I can love people in my church, and **please** give me ways to share with people in my church.
Help us be one big family, loving you together! Amen.

Philip and the Ethiopian

Philip met a man who was reading Isaiah's message from God, but couldn't understand who it was talking about. Philip explained that it was all about Jesus, God's promise-keeping, rescuing king. The Ethiopian wanted to live with Jesus as his king. Philip baptized him.

"The [Ethiopian] said to Philip, 'Please tell me, who is the prophet talking about?' ... Philip began to speak. He started with this same Scripture and told the man the Good News about Jesus." (Acts 8:34-35)

Dear God,
Thank you that every word of the Bible comes from you.
Thank you that every part of the Bible tells us how amazing King Jesus is.
Thank you for the people who help me to understand the Bible, and that your Spirit helps me believe in Jesus as I read it.
Please help me to understand, believe, and be excited about the Bible every day. Amen.

The Road to Damascus

Paul REALLY did not like Jesus and his friends. But when he was on the road to the city of Damascus, Jesus appeared to Paul. Now, Paul loved Jesus and his people. He wanted to tell everyone how great Jesus is!

Paul wrote, "Christ Jesus came into the world to save sinners. And I am the worst of those sinners. But I was given mercy." (1 Timothy 1:15-16)

Dear Jesus,
Thank you that you are so powerful that you can turn anyone into your friend.
Thank you that you are so kind that you wanted someone like Paul to be your friend.
Jesus, there are people I know who are not friends with you.
Please cause them to realize the truth about you.
Please give me someone to talk to today about how powerful and kind you are. Amen.

The One Who Keeps God's Promises

Paul and Barnabas told people about Jesus. They told them that God had made lots of promises, and that Jesus is the way that God keeps all of them. Some people believed their message, and became Christians. Others really did not like the message.

"We tell you the Good News about the promise God made to our ancestors … God has made this promise come true for us. God did this by raising Jesus from death."

(Acts 13:32-33)

Dear God,
Thank you for all your unbreakable promises: for your promise to forgive your people,
Your promise that your people will live in your perfect place forever,
And your promise that we will know happiness as we live under your king's rule.
Dear Jesus,
Thank you that you are the way all these promises are kept. You are our king. We love you. Amen.

Jesus's Friends in Philippi

In the city of Philippi, a rich woman and a slave-girl started to follow Jesus as their king. Then Paul and Silas met a prison guard. They told him how to be rescued and forgiven, and he became a Christian too.

"Believe in the Lord Jesus and you will be saved." (Acts 16:31)

Dear God,

Thank you that anyone can be saved and live with you forever if they believe in Jesus – including me!

Thank you that as long as I believe in Jesus, you will always love me and forgive me.

Sometimes I feel sad because things have gone wrong. **Please** remind me that you always love me.

Sometimes I feel bad because I have done something wrong. **Please** remind me that you always forgive me.

Amen.

Paul in Jerusalem and Rome

Some people did not like the message about Jesus that Paul was telling everyone he met. They put Paul in prison. In the end, Paul was taken to Rome. And everywhere he went, Paul kept telling everyone he could about Jesus.

"[Paul] preached about the kingdom of God and taught about the Lord Jesus Christ. He was very bold, and no one stopped him." (Acts 28:31)

Dear God,
Thank you that you are in charge of everything – even when it feels that things are going wrong, and even when people do not want to love Jesus.
Thank you for giving us the same job that Paul had – to tell everyone we can, everywhere we go, about Jesus.
Thank you for the places I go and the people I meet.
Please make me brave, so that I can tell people that Jesus loves them and wants to forgive them so that they can live with him forever. Amen.

Paul's Letters

The groups of people who wanted to live with Jesus as their king were called churches. Paul wrote letters to lots of the churches to remind them how much Jesus loved them and to teach them how to obey him.

"The important thing is faith – the kind of faith that works through love." (Galatians 5:6)

Dear God,
Thank you that your Holy Spirit told Paul what to write in his letters.
Please keep giving us faith to believe that Jesus is the king who keeps all your promises, the king who gives us life forever with you.
Thank you that we can show others how much you love them in the way that we love them.
Please show me how to treat my family and play with my friends in ways that are loving and kind. Amen.

More Letters

Several of Jesus's friends wrote letters to churches, just like Paul did. They reminded Jesus's followers that God really, really loved them; to keep believing in Jesus even when life was hard; that we show we are Jesus's friends by trying to obey him; and that Jesus is the best.

"The Father has loved us so much! He loved us so much that we are called children of God."

(1 John 3:1)

Dear Father,

Thank you for all the different people who you guided to write the different books of the Bible.

Thank you that you love us so much that we can't come up with words to describe how big your love is.

Thank you that you always and only do what you know is best for us.

Please help us to remember this when things are hard or make us sad.

You love us. And we love you, God. Amen.

In the middle of heaven, King Jesus is sitting on his throne. Around him are so many people they can't be counted. They speak every language there is and come from every country there is. They are praising Jesus. And so are millions of angels and animals and sea creatures.

"The Lamb who was killed is worthy to receive power, wealth, wisdom and strength, honor, glory, and praise!" (Revelation 5:12)

Dear Jesus,
We can't see heaven, so thank you for telling us what it is like there right now.
We praise you for ruling over everything. **Wow!**
We praise you that one day we will be there, standing round your throne. **Wow!**
Thank you that whenever we sing songs praising you, we're joining in with all those people in heaven.
Please keep us living with you as our king, all the way until we get to your throne. Amen.

I Am Coming Soon

One day, Jesus will get rid of the devil so that nothing can go wrong ever again. He will come back to this world, and everyone who loves Jesus as their king will live with him. Everything will be perfect and everyone will be perfect.

"Jesus is the One who says that these things are true. Now he says, 'Yes, I am coming soon.'"

(Revelation 22:20)

Dear Jesus,
Thank you that you are coming back. It is very exciting!
Thank you that you will get rid of the devil and remake this world to be perfect.
Thank you that, because you always keep all your promises, I know for sure that this will happen.
Jesus, **please** come back today. And if today isn't the day for you to come back, please keep me loving you as my king and remembering all your promises.
Amen.

GOD'S BIG PROMISES

Bedtime
Prayers

God Doesn't Sleep

"He who guards you never sleeps.
He who guards Israel
never rests or sleeps."

(Psalm 121:3-4)

Dear God,
You made everything, and you made me.
You care for everything, and you care for me.
You never sleep, and so you can guard me while I sleep.
Thank you that I can close my eyes, knowing you will
look after me all through the night.
As I drift off to sleep now, **please** give my heart peace
and my body rest.
Amen.

God Watches Over Me

"I will pray to the Lord.
 And he will answer me from his
 holy mountain.
I can lie down and go to sleep.
 And I will wake up again
 because the Lord protects me."

(Psalm 3:4-5)

Dear God,
Sometimes I find it hard to go to sleep.
But I know that you will look after me. I know that you
will listen to me.
I know that when I open my eyes in the morning, I'll be
in a new day that you have made for me – a new day
for me to love you and enjoy your world.
So I'm going to close my eyes now. I'm going to lie down
and go to sleep. **Thank you** that you will watch over
me till morning.
Amen.

Jesus Keeps Me Safe

"I go to bed and sleep in peace.
Lord, only you keep me safe."

(Psalm 4:8)

Dear Jesus,
You made the stars and you calmed a storm. You healed the sick and you helped the weak.
You can keep me safe tonight.
Thank you that I can go to bed and sleep in peace.
Thank you that you are with me, and that you will keep watch over me.
Thank you, Jesus.
Amen.

God Made Day and Night

"Then God said, 'Let there be light!' And there was light. God saw that the light was good. So he divided the light from the darkness. God named the light 'day' and the darkness 'night.'" (Genesis 1:3-5)

Dear God,
You made day and you made night.
Thank you for today. **Thank you** that it was light, to help me see. **Thank you** for all the things I've done and all the people I've seen.
Thank you for tonight. **Thank you** that it's dark, to help me sleep. **Thank you** for the rest that my mind and body will have.
And **thank you** that tomorrow it will be light again, and I'll be ready to enjoy another day in your world.
Amen.

You Are With Me

"The Lord is my shepherd...
Even if I walk
through a very dark valley,
I will not be afraid
because you are with me."

(Psalm 23:1,4)

Dear Jesus,
Sometimes, I don't much like the dark at nighttime.
Thank you that, however dark it is and however I feel, you are with me.
Thank you that I don't need to be afraid, because you are here.
Tonight, if I don't much like the dark, **please** remind me to say to you in my head:
You are with me.
You are with me.
You are with me.
Amen.

Our King and Shepherd

"Don't fear, little flock. Your Father
wants to give you the kingdom."

(Luke 12:32)

Dear Jesus,
Thank you for giving me a place in your kingdom, with
you ruling over me.
Thank you for making me a part of your flock, with
you looking after me.
Thank you that I can go to sleep tonight knowing that
you care for me and that you love me.
As I lie here in my bed, I am in your kingdom and I am
in your flock.
Please give me peace and sleep tonight, Lord Jesus.
Amen.

Jesus Gives Us Peace

"My peace I give you. I do not give it
to you as the world does. So don't
let your hearts be troubled."

(John 14:27)

Lord Jesus,
There are some things in this world that make us sad.
There are some things in this world that make us scared.
Thank you that you know about all those things, that
you are more powerful than all those things, and that
you came to give us peace.
Thank you that whatever tonight and tomorrow bring,
you will love me and look after me.
As I close my eyes, **please** let my heart feel your peace.
Amen.

Thank You for Today

"This is the day that the Lord has made. Let us rejoice and be glad today!" (Psalm 118:24)

Dear God,

Thank you for the day that is ending. You made it as a gift.

Thank you for the fun we've had and the food we've eaten and the friends we've seen. **Thank you**, God, for everything.

Thank you for the day that will come tomorrow. You will give it as a gift.

Thank you that you have planned it all out already. In between today and tomorrow comes tonight. **Thank you** for this time to rest.

Please give us the sleep we need, ready to enjoy tomorrow.

Amen.

Loved and Forgiven
(a Bedtime Sorry Prayer)

"As high as the sky is above the earth,
so great is his love for those who
respect him.
He has taken our sins away from us
as far as the east is from west."

(Psalm 103:11-12)

Dear God,
Thank you for today. We have done some good things and enjoyed some fun things.
But we know that we have also done some wrong things. We can think of times today when we have not loved and obeyed you. We are **sorry**.
Thank you that you take our sins and put them as far away from us as we could imagine.
Thank you that you do this because your love for us is bigger than we can imagine.
Thank you that as we go to sleep tonight, we are loved and we are forgiven.
Amen.

INDEX

GOD'S **BIG** PROMISES

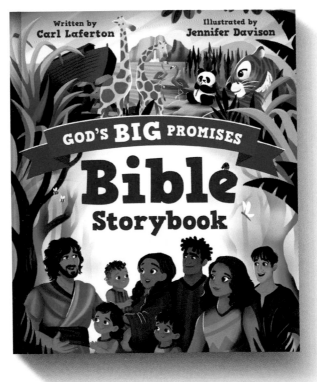

Written by
Carl Laferton

Illustrated by
Jennifer Davison

GOD'S **BIG** PROMISES

Bible
Storybook

92 foundational stories faithfully told, showing
how the Bible is one big story of God making and
keeping his promises. Perfect for using alongside
God's Big Promises Bible Story Prayers.

godsbigpromises.com

GOD'S BIG PROMISES
Family
Resources

Sticker and Activity Books

Board Books   Advent Devotions

godsbigpromises.com

Also by Carl Laferton

This best-selling 32-page storybook takes children on a journey from the Garden of Eden to God's perfect new creation. Kids aged 3-6 will learn why Jesus died and rose again, and why it's the best news ever.

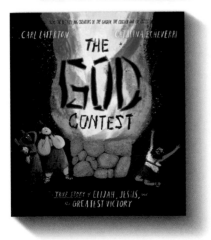

This award-winning book tells the gripping story of how the God of the Bible proved himself to be the one true God in the time of Elijah – and how he did so again, supremely, by raising Jesus from the dead.

thegoodbook.com | co.uk

thegoodbook
COMPANY

BIBLICAL | RELEVANT | ACCESSIBLE

At The Good Book Company, we are dedicated to helping Christians and local churches grow. We believe that God's growth process always starts with hearing clearly what he has said to us through his timeless word—the Bible.

Ever since we opened our doors in 1991, we have been striving to produce Bible-based resources that bring glory to God. We have grown to become an international provider of user-friendly resources to the Christian community, with believers of all backgrounds and denominations using our books, Bible studies, devotionals, evangelistic resources, and DVD-based courses.

We want to equip ordinary Christians to live for Christ day by day, and churches to grow in their knowledge of God, their love for one another, and the effectiveness of their outreach.

Call us for a discussion of your needs or visit one of our local websites for more information on the resources and services we provide.

Your friends at The Good Book Company

thegoodbook.com | thegoodbook.co.uk
thegoodbook.com.au | thegoodbook.co.nz
thegoodbook.co.in